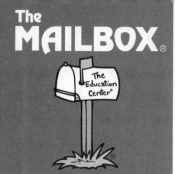

The MAILBOX®

The Education Center®

Sort All Sorts

K

MW01130219

115 Picture- and Word- Categorizing Activities

★ **Literacy Sorts**   ★ **Math Sorts**

★ **Science Sorts**   ★ **Social Studies Sorts**

Managing Editor: Tina Petersen

Editorial Team: Becky S. Andrews, Diane Badden, Kimberley Bruck, Karen A. Brudnak, Pam Crane, Lynn Drolet, Sarah Foreman, Tazmen Hansen, Marsha Heim, Lori Z. Henry, Debra Liverman, Kitty Lowrance, Jennifer Nunn, Mark Rainey, Greg D. Rieves, Hope Rodgers, Donna K. Teal, Rachael Traylor, Sharon M. Tresino, Zane Williard

Plus tips and tools for sorting!

www.themailbox.com

©2010 The Mailbox® Books
All rights reserved.
ISBN10 #1-56234-948-1 • ISBN13 #978-1-56234-948-6

Printed in the United States
10 9 8 7 6 5 4 3 2 1

HPS 215488

Table of Contents

ĕ as in

Math Sorts

Science Sorts

Social Studies Sorts

Sorting Tools

What's

Sort 24: Initial Consonants

V 🦺	W ⌚

Picture Sorts

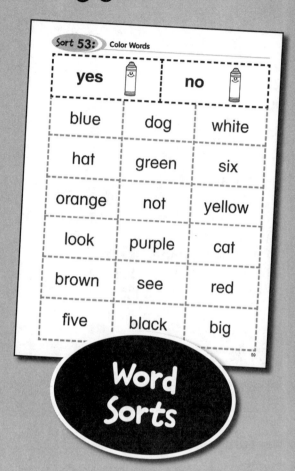

Sort 53: Color Words

yes 🖍		no 🖍
blue	dog	white
hat	green	six
orange	not	yellow
look	purple	cat
brown	see	red
five	black	big

Word Sorts

Sorts for...

Literacy

Math

Science

Social Studies

Inside

Picture and Word Sorts

Programmable Sorts

Sorting Mats

Handy Tips See page 6.

Storage

Handy Sorting Tips

For a quick center activity, put a laminated sort inside a gift bag.

For easy identification, have students glue each category card on a slightly larger construction paper rectangle.

Use the handy envelope pattern on page 128 to make storage envelopes. Additional storage options include business-size envelopes, resealable plastic bags, and string-tie envelopes.

Copy sorts onto colorful paper for added interest. Or use colorful paper to color-code sorts by curriculum area. For example, use white for literacy, yellow for math, green for science, and blue for social studies.

Use a variety of sorting activities, such as the following:

Closed sort: A student sorts the cards into the provided categories.

Open sort: Category cards are removed. A student looks for similarities among his cards and sorts them accordingly. Because open sorts often result in a variety of outcomes, allow time for students to explain their sorts.

Partner sort: A student works with a partner to complete an open or a closed sort.

Blind sort: For this auditory sort, display the category cards. Then name each of the remaining picture or word cards. Have students point to, name, or signal the appropriate category for each card.

Speed sort: This is a timed closed sort. Over several days, a student works to decrease the amount of time it takes to accurately complete a sort. This type of sort promotes speed with accuracy and should only be used to encourage automatic recognition.

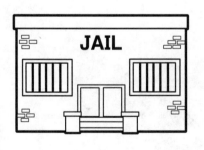

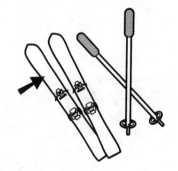

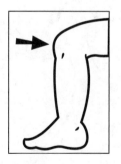

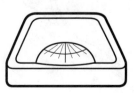

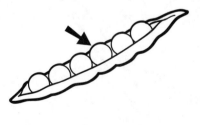

Rhyming

  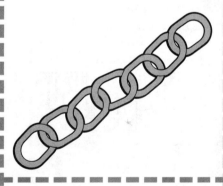

Sort 3: Rhyming

 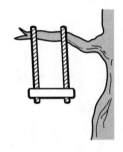 

  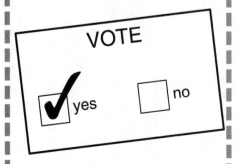

VOTE

✓ yes   ☐ no

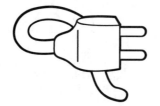

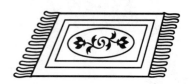

Rhyming

 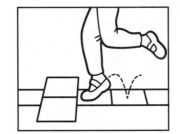 

  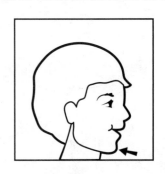

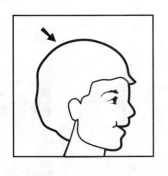  

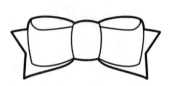

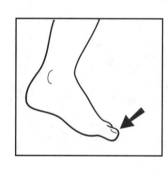

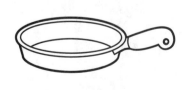

Sort 7: Syllables

Sort 8: Syllables

2	3

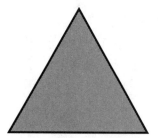

Sorts of All Sorts • ©The Mailbox® Books • TEC61266

Sort 9: Syllables

1	2	3

letter    number

7	R	5
B	3	F
8	M	4
Z	6	X

Aa	Gg

a	G	g
A	g	A
G	a	G
a	g	A

Jj	**Qq**	**Rr**
Q	R	J
j	r	q
Q	J	R
r	q	j

Sorts of All Sorts • ©The Mailbox® Books • TEC61266

Ii	Mm	Yy
I	y	M
m	Y	i
Y	I	m
i	M	y

uppercase letter	lowercase letter 

H	d	t
I	N	h
T	k	D
n	L	K

Note to the teacher: Have a student sort the letters into the two categories; then have her match each lowercase letter to its uppercase letter.

uppercase letter 	lowercase letter 

F	R	q
E	M	f
U	r	u
Q	e	m

Note to the teacher: Have a student sort the letters into the two categories; then have her match each lowercase letter to its uppercase letter. 21

r 	no match

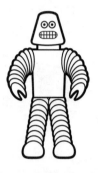  

Initial Consonants

S  | no match

  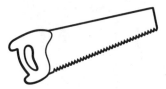

b    m

   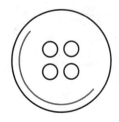   

     Sorts of All Sorts • ©The Mailbox® Books • TEC61266

p    t

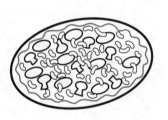   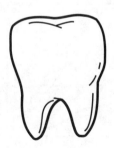   

f  | **g**

 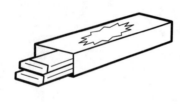 

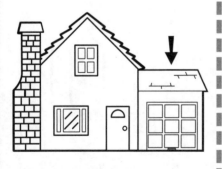 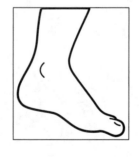 

c

n

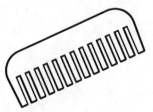

j

l

d  h

 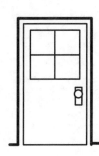 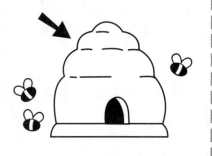

V 	W 

Initial Consonants

k 🗝	y 🧶	z 🦓

ends like  | no match

Sort 27: Ending Sounds

ends like

no match

ends like 	no match

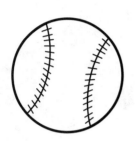  

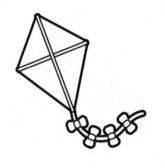  

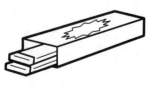  

Sort 29: Ending Sounds

ends like 	ends like 

  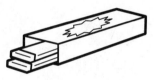

 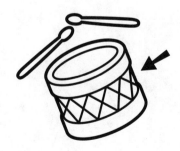 

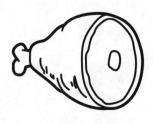  

ends like 	ends like 

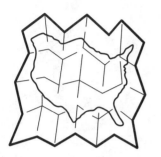

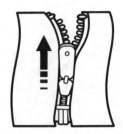

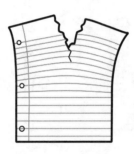

Sort 31: Ending Sounds

ends like  | ends like

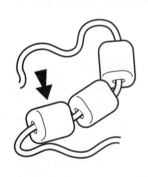  

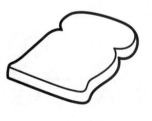  

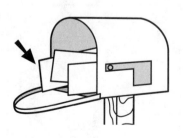  

ends like	ends like 

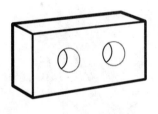  

  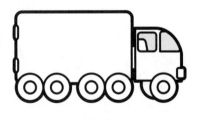

  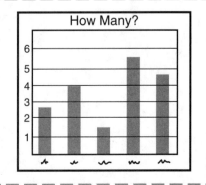

Sort 33: Ending Sounds

ends like    ends like

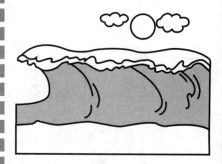

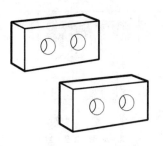

bug

pin

hug

fin

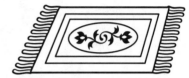

rug

grin

jug

win

mug

in

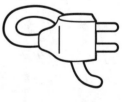

plug

twin

slug

chin

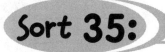

| m**ap**  | c**at**  |

cap

bat

clap

hat

nap

mat

wrap

rat

lap

Pat

snap

fat

b**ell**

h**ill**

fill

shell

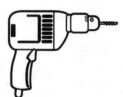

drill

smell

spell

bill

spill

well

grill

fell

pill

yell

bug    nut

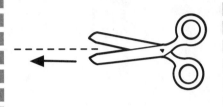      

jug   hut   hug

shut   rug   cut

Note to the teacher: Have a student sort the cards by their word families; then have her match each word to its picture.

mop

pot

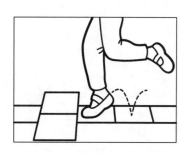

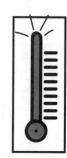

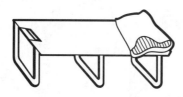

hot	pop	dot
top	cot	hop

Note to the teacher: Have a student sort the cards by their word families; then have him match each word to its picture.

fan

pin

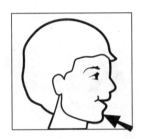

win

can

chin

man

fin

van

Note to the teacher: Have a student sort the cards by their word families; then have her match each word to its picture.

b**ed** 	p**en** 

red	hen	men
den	led	ten
fed	Ben	wed
sled	when	Ted

fl**ag** 	d**og** 

log	bag	fog
tag	hog	sag
clog	brag	frog
wag	jog	rag

cat

snail

nail

hat

pail

mat

quail

bat

mail

Pat

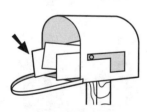

tail

rat

fat

sail

hill

slide

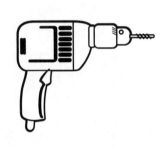

| drill | hide | spill |
| ride | fill | bride |

Note to the teacher: Have a student sort the cards by their word families; then have her match each word to its picture.

cap   **hay**

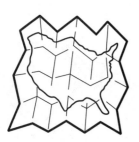      

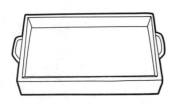      

map	tray	clap
pay	nap	play

cake   **gate**

lake

date

 *(rake)*

rake

skate

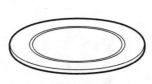

snake

state

shake

plate

bake

crate

wake

Nate

night

ice

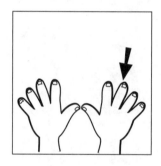

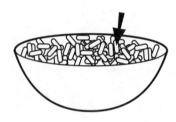

dice

light

mice

fight

rice

right

Note to the teacher: Have a student sort the cards by their word families; then have him match each word to its picture.

rain 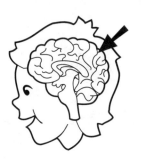   nine

_____

| line | chain | vine |
| brain | pine | drain |

Note to the teacher: Have a student sort the cards by their word families; then have her match each word to its picture.

53

ă as in  | ĭ as in

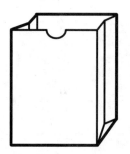

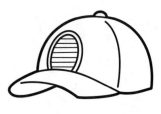

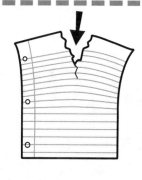

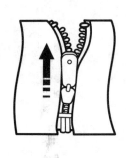

Sort 49: Short Vowels

ĕ as in 	ŏ as in 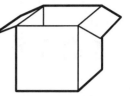

  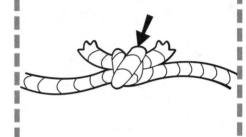

Sort 50:   Short Vowels

ĭ as in 	ŭ as in 

 pig	 rug	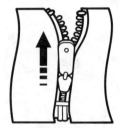 zip
 cup	 hit	 bug
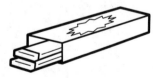 gum	 lip	 sun
 rip	 bun	 six

Sorts of All Sorts • ©The Mailbox® Books • TEC61266

Short Vowels

ă as in

ŏ as in

hat

fox

can

pop

map

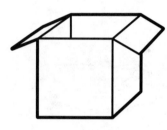

box

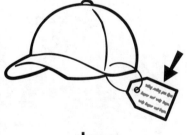

tag

rock

bat

log

van

pot

ĕ as in    **ŭ** as in

hug

pen

bus

jet

nut

wet

ten

bug

shell

run

web

cup

yes 	no 

blue	dog	white
hat	green	six
orange	not	yellow
look	purple	cat
brown	see	red
five	black	big

yes 	no 	
ten	two	and
me	have	three
four	of	nine
it	five	said
eight	like	six
go	seven	little

one	more than one

dog

crabs

frog

frogs

pig

bat

bugs

crab

dogs

pigs

bats

bug

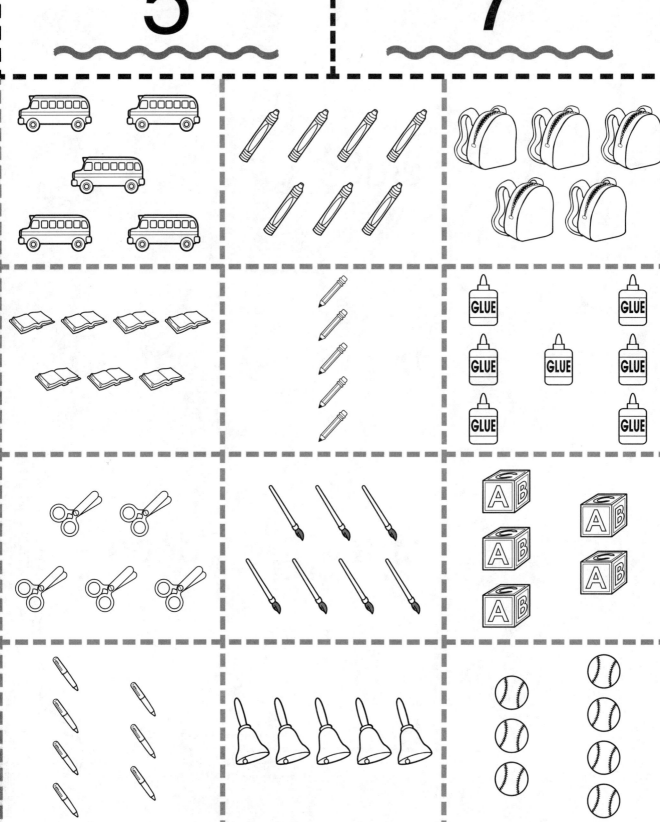

5

7

Sorts of All Sorts • ©The Mailbox® Books • TEC61266

Sort 57: Counting Sets

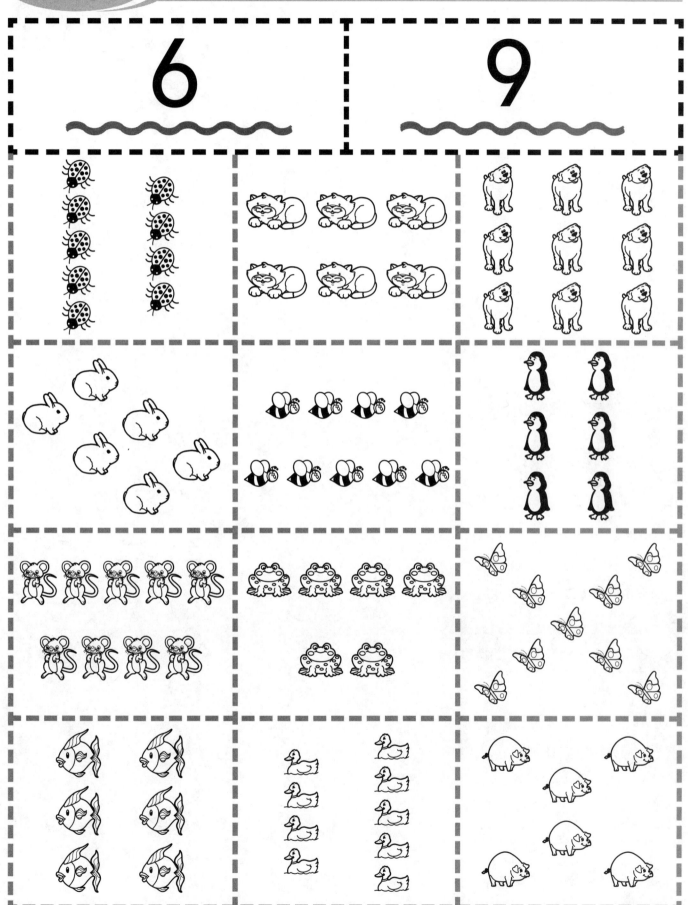

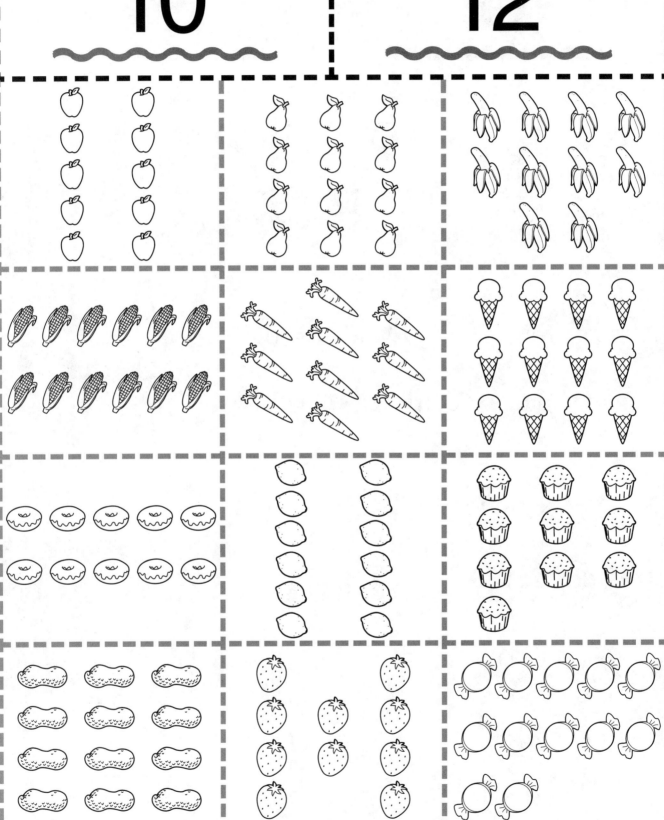

Sorts of All Sorts • ©The Mailbox® Books • TEC61266

2	4

  four

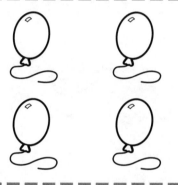  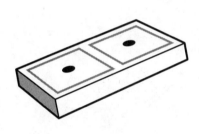

two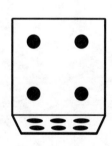

 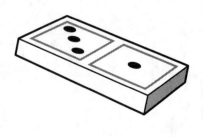 

5	10

ten
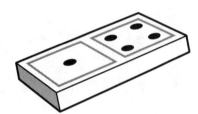

five

 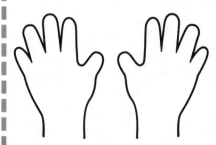 

less than 8	more than 8

less than 12	more than 12

less than 10	more than 10

5	13	2
~~	~~~~~~	~~~~~~
20	8	16
~~	~~~~~~	~~~~~~
9	17	3
~~	~~~~~~	~~~~~~
15	6	19
~~	~~~~~~	~~~~~~

less than 20	more than 20

22	15	26
9	24	7
28	12	21
10	29	18

Sorts of All Sorts • ©The Mailbox® Books • TEC61266

Sort 65: Positional Words

on	over	under

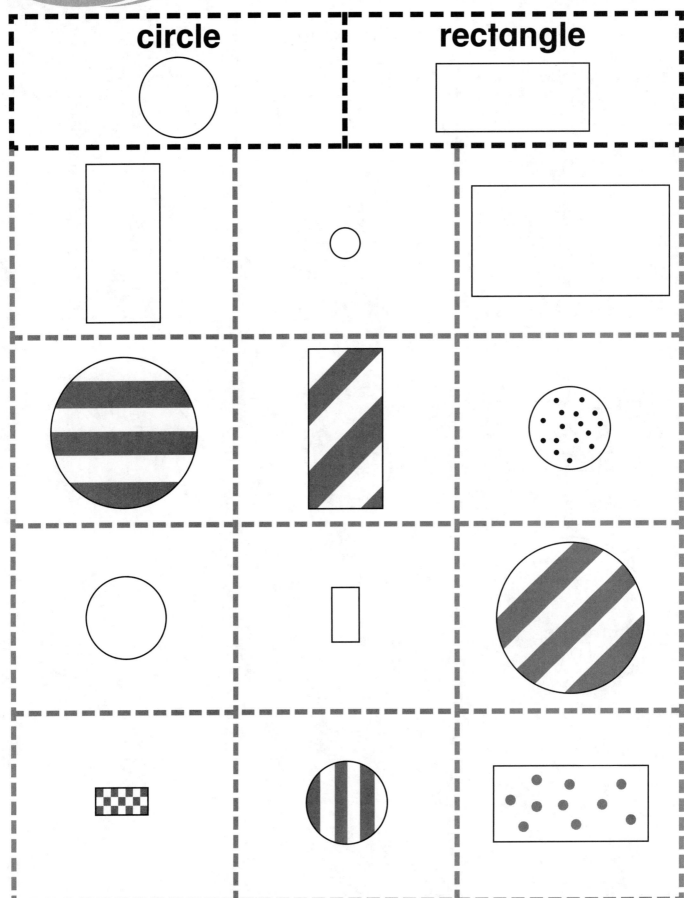

Plane Shapes

square	triangle	no match

Plane Shapes

circle	square	no match

Sorts of All Sorts • ©The Mailbox® Books • TEC61266

Sort 69: Plane Shapes and Solid Figures

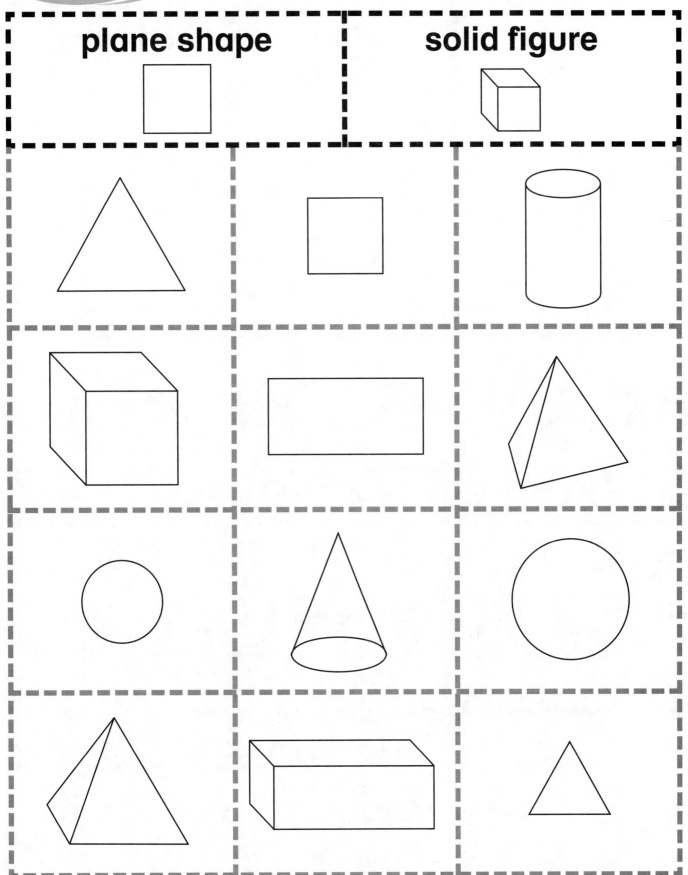

Note to the teacher: Have a student sort the cards by shapes and solids; then have him pair each shape to a solid with a matching face.

sphere	cylinder	no match

Sorts of All Sorts • ©The Mailbox® Books • TEC61266

Sort 71: Solid Figures

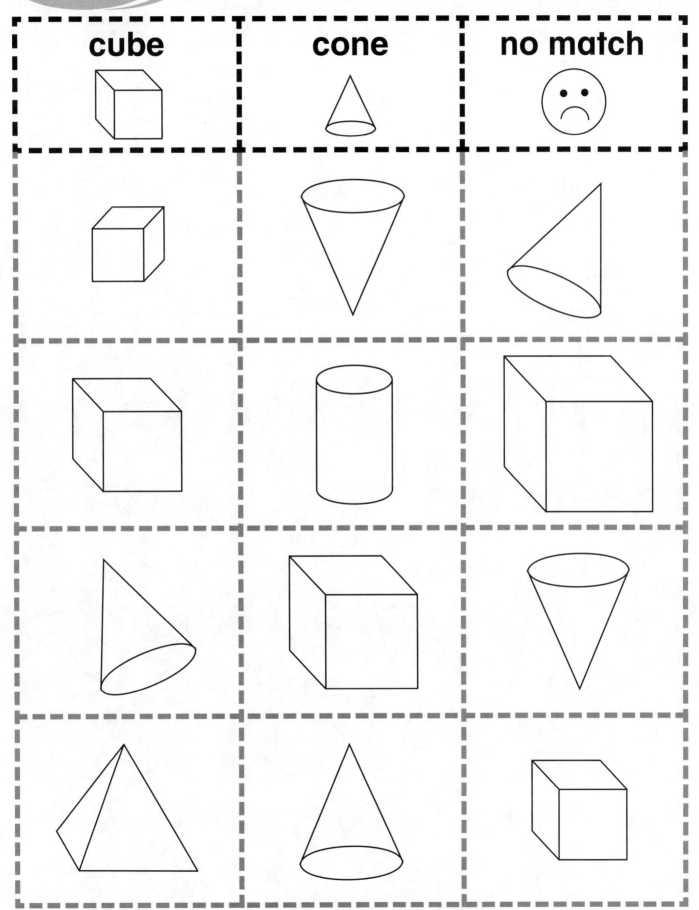

Sort 72: Solid Figures

sphere	cube	cone

Sorts of All Sorts • ©The Mailbox® Books • TEC61266

Sort 73: Measurement

taller than 	shorter than 

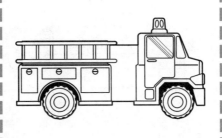

heavy    light

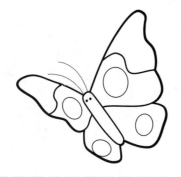      

day    **night**

Sort 76: Time

more time than	less time than

	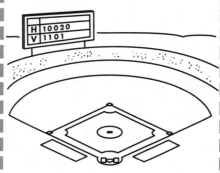	

Sort 77: Time

analog clock 	digital clock 

Sorts of All Sorts • ©The Mailbox® Books • TEC61266

Note to the teacher: Have a student sort the clocks; then have her match each digital clock to an analog clock.

equal 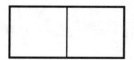   not equal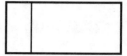

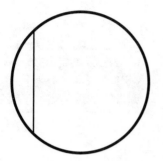

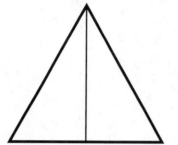

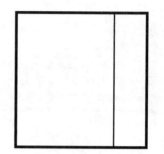

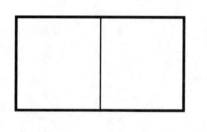

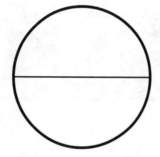

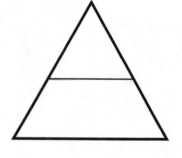

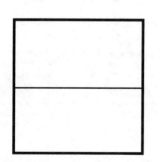

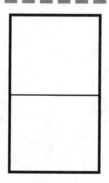

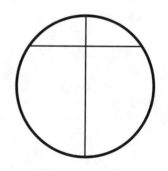

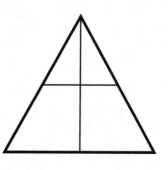

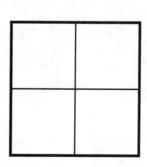

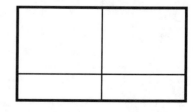

Sort 79: Fractions

| equal | not equal |

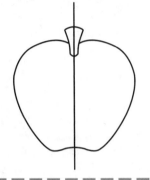

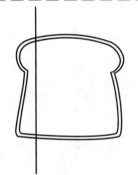

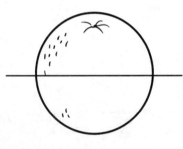

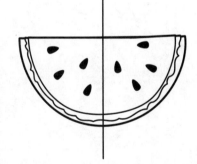

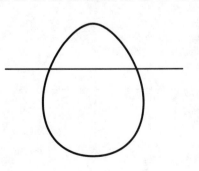

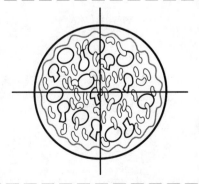

wholes	halves	fourths

Sorts of All Sorts • ©The Mailbox® Books • TEC61266

Sort 81: Fractions

fourths

no match

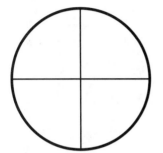

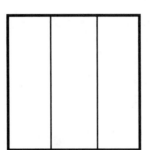

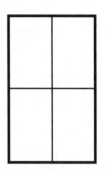

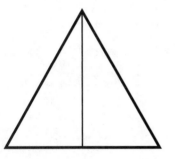

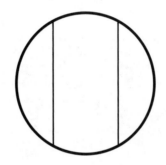

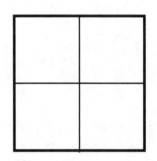

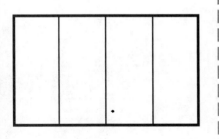

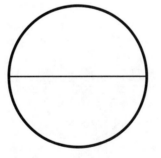

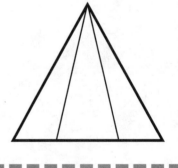

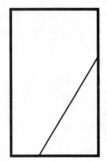

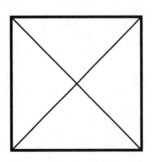

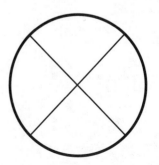

Sort 82: Coins

penny	dime

Sort 83: Coins

penny	nickel

penny	nickel	dime

Sort 85: Coins

10¢	20¢

less than 10¢	more than 10¢

2	3	4

5	7

1 + 4

1 + 6

4 + 1

4 + 3

2 + 3

5 + 2

0 + 5

7 + 0

3 + 4

3 + 2

2 + 5

5 + 0

Sort 89: Addition

9	10

5 + 4

2 + 8

7 + 3

8 + 1

2 + 7

1 + 9

5 + 5

3 + 6

0 + 9

4 + 6

8 + 2

7 + 2

4	5	6
4 + 0	2 + 3	5 + 1
0 + 5	2 + 2	4 + 1
3 + 3	3 + 2	3 + 1
1 + 3	2 + 4	6 + 0

Sort 91: Subtraction

correct	not correct

$4 - 2 = 2$

$3 - 1 = 1$

$5 - 1 = 4$

$2 - 0 = 0$

$2 - 1 = 1$

$4 - 3 = 2$

$5 - 3 = 2$

$5 - 2 = 2$

$3 - 0 = 3$

$3 - 2 = 2$

$4 - 4 = 0$

$5 - 5 = 5$

Sort 92: **Subtraction**

correct	not correct

8 – 4 = 5	6 – 2 = 4	9 – 6 = 4

7 – 3 = 4	10 – 6 = 6	8 – 7 = 1

6 – 0 = 0	9 – 5 = 4	10 – 9 = 2

10 – 5 = 5	8 – 2 = 5	7 – 7 = 0

eat    do not eat

  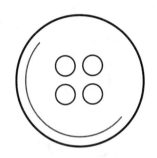

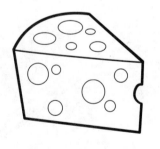  

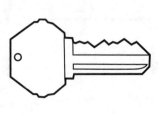  

touch

do not touch

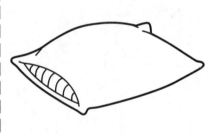

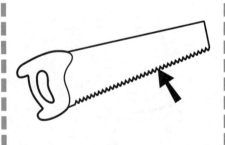

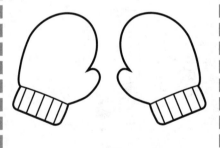

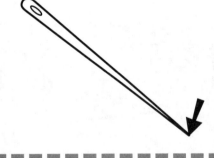

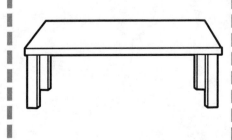

Sort 95: Five Senses—Smell

has a smell	has no smell 

 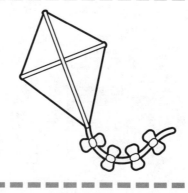 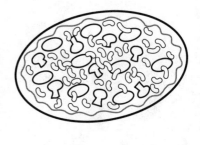

can hear | cannot hear

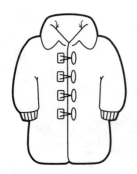

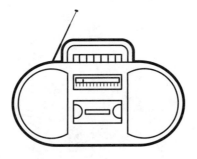

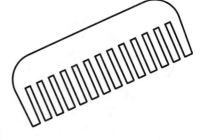

Sort 97: Five Senses—Sight

| green | red | yellow |

Sort 98: Living or Nonliving

living 	nonliving

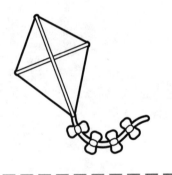  

Sort 99: Animals

legs	no legs 

| fly  | cannot fly  |

Sorts of All Sorts • ©The Mailbox® Books • TEC61266

lives on land	lives in ocean

Sort 102: Animals

adult

baby

Note to the teacher: Have a student sort the animals; then have him match each baby animal to the matching adult animal.

rain  | snow

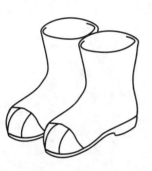

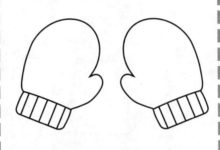

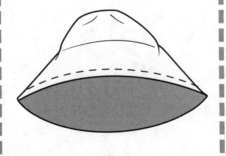

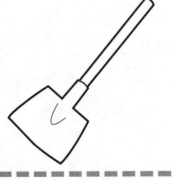

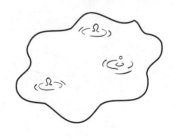

hot   cold

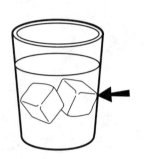

Sorts of All Sorts • ©The Mailbox® Books • TEC61266

Sort 105: Seasons

summer clothes	winter clothes

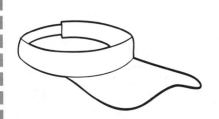

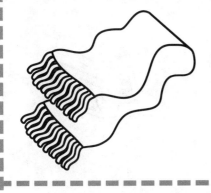

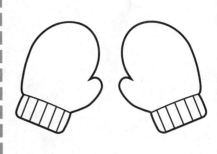

Sort 106: Seasons

summer	fall	winter

Sorts of All Sorts • ©The Mailbox® Books • TEC61266

Sort 107: Plants

grows on a plant	does not grow on a plant

Sort 108: Plants

| a plant need  | not a plant need  |

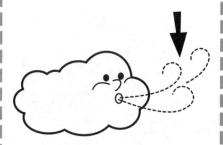

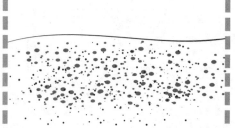

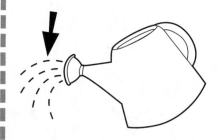

Sort 109: Community

home	community

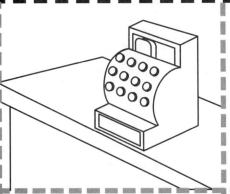 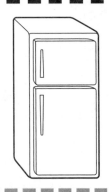 

 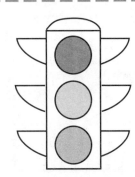 

  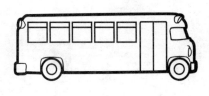

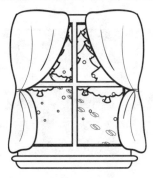  

teacher	dentist

GLUE

COLORFUL CRAYONS

Toothpaste

A

B

C

Mouthwash

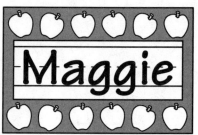

Maggie

Sort 111: Community Helpers

doctor	police officer	custodian

firefighter	farmer	mail carrier

Sorts of All Sorts • ©The Mailbox® Books • TEC61266

Sort 113: Transportation

land	air	water

needs	wants

  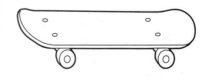

Sort 115: Environment

good	bad

Programmable Sort:

Sorts of All Sorts • ©The Mailbox® Books • TEC61266

Programmable Sort:

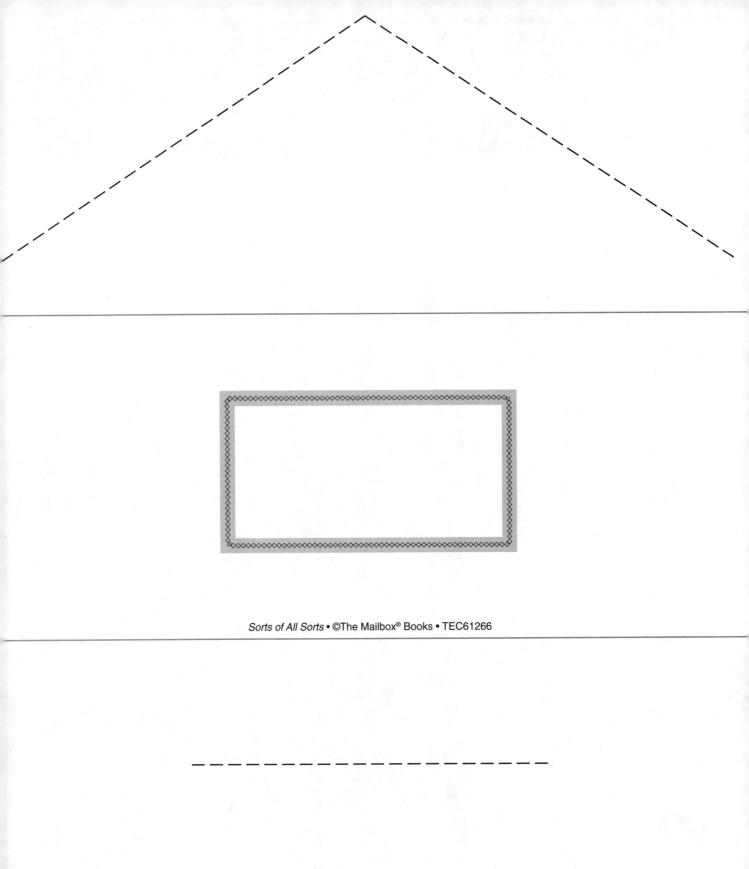

Sorts of All Sorts • ©The Mailbox® Books • TEC61266

Envelope Pattern: To make a storage envelope, copy this page and cut on the dotted lines. Fold along the bottom solid line (keeping the programming to the outside) and seal the left and right edges with glue. To close the envelope, fold the triangular flap down and tuck it into the slit.

128